Dreamin' Your Leadership

Elise A.C. Ledderhof

Dedicated, in Loving Memory, to my Father:

†12-02-2012

CONTENTS

SOME NOTES TO THE READER

Every single person has built up a certain amount of baggage during their lives. Some of this is useful and needs to be held onto forever, other parts have become a huge burden. I want to ask you if you are aware of any of these burdens, better known as survival mechanisms or mindsets. Some of these mindsets are helpful others will work against you.

This book is about a journey during which we become aware of events from our past having a lasting effect on us, such as slowing us down. We find out that we do not have to lead our lives the way we do because of these events. On the contrary, we can decide right now to see things in a new perspective and start acting accordingly from now on, forever more.

In order to make this a success, it's important to become aware of everything that's holding us back and what it is we need in order to achieve what it is we want to be or do. Let us take a closer look at our goals and the reasons behind these goals. Is this a goal that's supporting you or is it a result of unfortunate circumstances and not helping you out at all?

To help you reconnect to your inner child and relive your unconscious memories, a lot of expressive language has been used, with the purpose of having emotions and feelings resurface again. Every person will have a different journey, since everyone has had a different walk of life. Some of you might enjoy travelling by train and will always use the same routes. Others of you might abandon these tracks and start to fly and view the world from a bird's eye view. Maybe you'll make this journey on foot, so you can absorb everything in your own time and in your own pace. Whatever your choice might be, it's about experiencing and living this journey and then becoming aware of how this will help you in your life to come.

Enjoy!

Elise

INTRODUCTION

This book consists of two parts. The First part is a story about "A Journey ToThe Stars". It tells about someone having a dream and deciding to act upon this dream, after reading a newspaper clipping which tells about the dream. This person decides to go on a journey and during this trip gets to meet a lot of different people. These people all play a role in explaining the events during this trip and especially the meaning behind these events.

Part two explains the journey step by step. What do the various signals mean? How do our brains work with regards to memories and survival mechanisms? Do we still want to act according to our programs (mindsets) or would we like to start changing things? If so, how do we do so?

This book will have a follow-up in the form of a workbook. This workbook will help people work out their dreams, mindsets and possible changes when being at home.

This book is part of the course "Dreamin' Your Leadership". If you're curious about the course or if you want more information, please go to www.ChikaraCC.com.

PART ONE

Journey to the Stars

1. A DREAM

"Choo Choo… Choo Choo…" What is it I'm hearing? "Vreeeeeeeeeeeeew vreeeeeeeeeeeeeeew". I now hear a whistle… While looking around me I start to realise I'm sitting inside a steam train.

The sound of the whistle is being heard yet again. The driver is sending a warning signal. Before I can think about this, I'm being pushed into the couch. My eyes are wide open when I see what's happening. We are taking off into the air! How's that possible? With what seems to be an incredible speed we're heading for the stars. I feel like I'm in Disneyland, inside one of those attractions that's shooting me straight into space! Just as suddenly as we rushed off towards the stars, we're slowing down and I'm trying to catch my breath. Before I know what's happening, we're moving once again. This time we're moving at a slower pace.

We are now moving right between the stars and when I look closely I can see all sorts of keys. Every time we stop at a key, someone's name is being called. Suddenly it's my name being called.

Before I have the time to respond properly I hear an instruction "On your right-hand side you can find the key to your dreams. Please walk to the window on your right, open it and get your key. You can recognise that it's yours by the way it sparkles and shines.

The sparkling and shining are the signs that it's your key ready to help you out. Once I walk over I can see it's a real key. I roll down the window and fetch it. While in my hand the key starts to shine soft colours, as if representing the warmth of my hand. Next I wake up. I'm lying in my bed and when looking at my pillow I can see the print of a key. What does this mean?

2. NEWSPAPER CLIPPING

While having breakfast, my attention gets drawn to an article in the newspaper. It tells about stars looking like keys. It continues by stating that last night numerous events like these occurred, but there hasn't been any solid evidence for these keys. For some unknown reason the keys haven't shown on the pictures, or on the videos, only the stars are visible. However, it was particularly bright last night.

Whilst reading on, I spot a tiny advertisement. Stars are surrounding the ad and in the midst of it is a keyhole. The text from the ad says: "Find the way to the key, which will take you to your dreams. For more instructions please go to the nearest beach at one o' clock this afternoon. These instructions will lead you to the meeting point "Station to the Stars" ".

I suddenly realise I only have a few hours left to prepare for this event. When I want to reread the instructions they are gone. That's strange. The ad has disappeared. I do however decide to go there. One thing is for certain: I can't and won't ignore signals like these.

3. THE BEACH

The nearest beach…That's actually the beach I prefer going to. And what was supposed to be there?

I haven't got anything to loose. I do have everything to gain by going there. I have felt uneasy and restless for a while now. It's like I want to change things, but I'm just not sure how to. Maybe going there will help me find out what it is I'd like to do. Even if I wouldn't get any answers I would still enjoy the peace and quiet from the sea. There's nothing beyond the sound of the waves and the salty smell of the ocean.

While walking towards the beach, I'm getting a slight awkward feeling in my tummy. It consists of a mixture of both tension and feeling of being nauseous. The feeling reminds me of that specific moment just before having an interview for a job I want really badly. Then again, I'm not going for an interview, I'm going to the beach. So what's this feeling trying to tell me?

I'm walking towards the stairs and start going down the steps, one at a time. It's a wooden staircase with the steps covered in sand. Since I can hardly see the steps I need to focus on walking. Every now and then I do look up, and it seems like I'm spotting something in the distance close to the ocean. I can't look long enough to find out what it is since I need to pay close attention to the steps, but it's long enough to make me at least a bit curious.

I'm getting more and more excited. Could it be true? What was it I'd been reading in that newspaper? "More instructions can be found on the nearest beach". Well, that's most certainly this beach. Besides telling me there would be directions to a station, there wasn't much more information to go on.

Thinking back to the dream and the newspaper clipping about the stars resembling keys, I'm realizing that this is too good to be true. Could this really become a reality? And if so, what would the meaning be behind this key? Vaguely I remember something about “being helped”. I might be helped out by this key. But how? The more I think about this, the less sense it seems to make.

I’m getting close to the coastline now, having crossed the beach almost completely, when something suddenly catches my eye. There it is, right in front of me, moving in the wind. There is so much movement going on I can’t keep my eyes off it. But what is “it”?

4. A TREASURE MAP ON CANVAS

When entering the pile of sand, there's something sticking out of this pile. I use my hand to wipe away the sand and I discover it's a piece of fabric, the size of a big handkerchief. It feels very special, like silk. Why would someone leave behind such a beautiful piece of fabric? Maybe someone has lost it. It sure looks precious and very carefully I pull it out of the pile of sand.

Being able to take a closer look I can now make out some sort of a drawing. Wiping the sand away from the drawing I see a steam train. There's a plate with the number "737" on it. I vaguely remember this being the same number as the number on the train in my dream. This most certainly can't be a coincidence.

Next I spot a sky full of stars on the drawing and right in the middle, between the stars, I can see a key shining and sparkling. This sends a shiver down my spine. I remember the newspaper article stating "Tonight numerous people have seen stars resembling keys".

Looking at the pile of sand I can tell there's something else stacked in there. It looks like some kind of box. What could this be?

5. THE COMPASS

Going through the sand I start to dig out a box that's round and on the cover seems to be an engraving. Looking closer I can distinguish it's a big polestar. Very carefully I try to open the box. The box is a little rusty and I'm afraid it will fall apart if I'm not careful enough. I'm completely taken by surprise, once I manage to open the box. There's all this light coming out of the tiny little box, as if it's trying to tell me something.

I close the box again quickly since the light is so bright it's actually blinding me. My hand is tightly wrapped around the box and I can feel the warmth coming from this tiny box. It makes me open my hand and take another look. I then notice that there's a similarity between the drawing on the silk canvas and the lid of the compass. Both contain the pole star showing what seem to be wind directions. The box in my hand is a compass. It's going to guide me on my path. That's something I'm very certain about!

Suddenly there's a firm breeze and as a result it's starting to cool off rather quickly. I decide to go back. While walking down the stairs I can feel the compass starting to heat up again in my hand. With the warmth comes the feeling of excitement deep within me. What's happening? Again I start remembering words "You'll be able to recognize the key by its bright and shiny sparkling. This will be your sign that this is your key, which will be helping you out in the near future." Then the words are changing: "You'll be able to recognize the compass by its bright and shiny sparkling. This will be helping you out in the near future". Helping me out? Helping me out how?

Before I get the chance to give it any further though I notice I'm standing before an old building. It's broken down over the years but it still has what seems to be a stately appearance. Back in the days it must have been an important building. Strange, I thought I knew every spot in these surroundings, but I most certain I've never been at this location.

6. THE STATION

When entering the building my attention is being drawn towards the big station clock. It's five o'clock. Five o'clock? That can't be right, so much time has passed. Maybe the clock has stopped working. When checking my phone it's showing me the exact same time. It really is five o'clock.

I decide to keep on walking. While walking through the rubble, amidst the broken walls filled with cracks, it seems very unrealistic there's a functioning station clock. Again the compass starts to glow within my hand. It is as if it wants to point out a certain direction. Should I turn left or right? When thinking of turning to the right I feel the compass glowing even more and I decide to take the turn to the right.

I can see I'm approaching a tunnel. Suddenly lights are turned on illuminating the tunnel and there's a message from the public address system sounding: "The train with destination "To the Stars" will arrive shortly on this platform. Please be sure to stay clear from the tracks, so no accidents can occur when the train arrives. Suction is very strong, so please stand back." I take a step back towards the railing, not a moment to soon, because I can feel the strong wind. An enormous dust cloud starts to appear and I turn away to protect myself from all the dust, rubble and dirt being caused by the arrival of the train on the platform.

7. A REAL STEAM TRAIN

After the dust clouds have disappeared, there's a huge surprise standing in front of me. It's a real steam train. A real big black monster surrounded by steam coming out of all of its pores. Wow, a real steam train in my neighbourhood. I just can't believe it.

Then I hear a voice: "Do you intend to hop along or do you want to stay here and watch? In a couple of minutes this train is about to take off to her destination to the stars. If you want to tag along, you'd better hurry". I'm looking at the man who, judging by his expression, seems to be feeling sorry for me. It's the ticket-collector, who now is shouting at his colleague, the engine driver: Henry, please come over here and help out a little! How on earth can we leave our guest standing here on the platform?" I'm looking past the ticket-collector to see the engine driver waving at me. He's got a huge smile on his face. "Well a big hello to you, our special guest! Welcome aboard our train. You know, this is a very special train. This train will help your dreams come to life. So again… be welcome!"

The steam train starts to huff and puff louder and louder. It's still at a hold, but the engine driver is busy preparing the boiler for the journey. I decide to step aboard the train, but then the ticket-collector asks me what I want to do with all my luggage. Looking around me, I'm surprised to see bags, suitcases and all this other stuff, serving as luggage. It's everything I have ever collected in my life. Never before have I seen this and to be honest, it's rather confrontational.

Not sure if it's a wise thing to be doing, I decide to take all of the luggage with me. I have to take a closer look first, before deciding what it is I do or do not want to bring along. This includes all this stuff I don't have a clue what it's used for. I'm starting to look for the manual or at least some document that will help me out in deciding what to keep and why. It turns out a number of things aren't of any value at all. In fact they're holding me back. This luggage is keeping me at the station and preventing me from getting on board the train.

What should I be doing? It's probably best if I leave some stuff behind. Is it a wise thing to do? Who can tell? It's impossible to take everything with me and it most certainly is not something to be desired. I should most definitely make a choice. Suddenly I'm aware I'm burning my hand. The compass has become immensely hot, forcing me to open my hand. The lid of the compass opens up, the moment I'm opening up my hand, followed by a melodious voice asking me a number of questions: "What's your purpose? What is it you want to achieve? What will you be needing in order to achieve this? What is it you'd like to leave behind for now and forever? This is your chance of a lifetime! Take it!"

I look up from the compass straight into the face of the ticket-collector with disbelief and surprise. The ticket-collector is laughing at me, then says to me: "You have to decide what luggage you want to bring along with you if you intend to come along with us. There's plenty of room for all of your stuff, but the more you take with you, the longer it will be before you'll arrive at your destination.

At that moment I cannot comprehend the truth of his statement. The next thing I know choices are made for me to leave behind part of my luggage. Henry, the engine driver starts to blow the whistle. If I want to come along I will have to leave some stuff behind. Now! I jump on the train before realizing I've randomly grabbed some suitcases and bags.

When the train starts to move I can see from a distance what it is I've left behind. Some of this stuff contains a lot of memories, not always the most positive ones. For a moment life seems harsh to me.

Then Marty, the ticket-collector, gives me a big wink. "So… how does it feel to be travelling a little lighter? Can you breathe easier after leaving all this stuff behind or is it still hard to grasp for you?" I'm looking at this guy. He's a slightly older man with a face that seems to be telling a thousand stories. His eyes stand out from his face. He's looking at me as if he's reading me, but at the same time there are sparkles in his eyes. I get a big smile from him. Next I realize a huge burden has been lifted from my shoulders. It's okay to let things be and leave them be. Especially when they are no longer needed.

8. A TICKET TO THE STARS

I'm getting installed in the train, enjoying the view, wondering about everything that has happened up 'till now, including the dream I had early this morning, What was it about? Ah, I remember. It was about being shot into the air. This train doesn't seem to be going at such a pace that something like this would be likely to happen, which actually is a good thing, considering it was already wild enough when happening in the dream!

After a while I get accompanied by Marty, the ticket-collector. He wants to know if I already feel a little bit better after all these commotions: "Things happened rather quickly, didn't they? But you know, it was a wise choice to go on this ride with us. These journeys to the stars are always very special and rest assured that you'll be going home a lot richer. No one will ever be able to take away this experience from you."

In the meantime Marty gives me my ticket. It's got the colour of sand and holds the picture of a compass. He's clipped out a mark, looking like a key. Right at that moment a message can be heard. They want Marty to come to the front of the train. Something must be going on. "Excuse me, but I need to go now. The train isn't picking up as much speed as it should be and I think they want to discuss this. You know, whenever people decide to bring all the luggage they can carry, it slows down the train immensely."

I can still hear his words in my mind, while Marty's walking off. I take a good look at all the luggage I've taken with me. This moment could be an excellent time to sort through all this stuff.

9. LONG LOST MEMORIES

One by one I take out all the bags and the suitcases from the rack. It seems like it's going on forever. While collecting all these bags I notice labels are attached to each item.

When looking more closely at the labels, it's like I'm watching short movies. Each label has got a movie of its own. I decide to watch one of these movies a little more closely. I install myself on the couch with the first one that catches my eye.

To my surprise I'm being taken back to a moment in time when I was still a young kid. "*I'm playing in the sandpit as suddenly other children come running up to me. They want to play in the sandpit, not considering at all that I'm already there, playing as well. Before I know it all my toys have been taken away from me and I'm left with nothing to play with anymore, except for the sand. I do not get the chance to think about this or react to it, because the next moment someone is picking me up from the sandpit and carrying me into the house, out of the sunshine. It feels like being punished for having those kids take away my toys!*"

I grab another suitcase. Again a movie is shown on the label. "*I'm at the playground in the schoolyard. In the midst of the playground is a magnificent device. It looks like a tiny little train and every time I start to move, it goes either from the left to the right or from the back to the front.*

I feel a rush going through my tiny body as I'm sitting in the train. This time however I do not get the chance to enter the train. All these kids are running past me, getting in before me. I feel like I've experienced this before, but I can't tell when this had happened.

At this moment all I can feel is frustration and disappointment. I wanted to get into that train and go onto a journey of dreams. Instead I have to look at these kids screaming and yelling at one another, pushing each other sideways in order to sit behind the wheel. When the bell rings all the kids rush off as quickly as they came running up here. I decide to go into the train, even if it's just for a little while. But when I try to get into the train I hear the clicks of my teacher's heels. She grabs me by the hand and tells me to go inside. I then realize I'd missed out on this amazing journey of dreams. It feels very sad, 'because it's like I've missed out on a wonderful opportunity. Instead I have to get back into the building, feeling robbed of all freedom."

A number of movies go by. Each of the movies contains memories of special moments being taken away from me; maybe I'm even being robbed of these moments. Could it be I let this happen to me? Looking at the suitcases they no longer seem that inviting to me. I feel like I've got a lump in my throat and there's a bitter taste in my mouth. Realizing this, the train starts to come to a halt. Again a message is being played. This time it's meant for me. They want to know what luggage is holding back the train from gaining speed. If we want to reach the stars, we can't afford to be held back.

At that moment I understand I do not want to be held back any longer by others. Before I know it I decide to get rid of these suitcases. Whether this message was truly meant for me or not, I'm going to take advantage of this opportunity to dump all this garbage. I'm never going to be held back anymore by anyone ever, unless I think it's a sensible and wise thing to do. From now on, I'm going for my own freedom!

10. SUPERFLUOUS BAGGAGE

Just above the window I can see a thick, cream-coloured cord. Attached to it is a second thick rope that's hanging along the window. Attached to this cord is a copper bell. The long cord is going straight to the walls of all cabins, forming a direct link with the engine-driver and the ticket-collector. I pull the cord and get startled for a moment because of the sudden sounds from all bells being rung in the entire train.

Fortunately for me Marty appears with a big wide smile on his face. "Have you made up your mind yet? You figured this out, didn't you? This message indeed was meant for you! How about burning this baggage altogether?" I feel my face is shining as I'm looking at him. This guy seems to know all my wishes! "Let's get all these bags to the engine-driver, Henry. He can burn them on the spot. How about that?"

The train now has come to a full top. We step out of the train and walk towards the front; to Henry. He opens up the hatch to the furnace and I put in my first suitcase. To my surprise the suitcase seems to be fitting the size of the hatch! At the same moment a big white flame appears, surrounded by numerous silver sparks. Then everything is back to normal again. The furnace is filled with charcoal again. "Want to do it one more time?" Henry asks me. I sure like this so I give him another bag. Again this incredible flame appears. This is wildly magnificent! Both men look at me with twinkles in their eyes. "What do you think Marty?" asks Henry. "This deserves something special, right? This is the next step when it comes to getting rid of all this garbage other people have left behind on your doorstep!"

Henry looks at me and asks me if I still have the treasure map. Of course I do! I pull the canvas very carefully out of my pocket. Henry takes the map and pins on a word: "Freedom". As soon as the word has been attached to the canvas, it starts to glow. At the same time so do I. I do not know who's more radiant, that pin or me, but my oh my… do I feel good about myself! "C'mon, let's return to your cabin. Let’s see if we can pick out some other bags that can be thrown away!”

While walking back, the train slowly starts to move again. There’s a noticeable difference in how rapidly the speed of the train starts to increase. My thoughts drift off when I’m sitting on the couch again. How great would it be if I could stand up for myself in a firm manner! I take another look at that pin with the word “Freedom”. I wonder what “freedom” represents for me. I pull out the writing tablet from the wall. I notice some words have already been written down on the paper on top of the tablet. “To me freedom is…”. I immediately start to write down:

- Standing up for myself;
- Continuing to do whatever it is I’m doing or planning to do;
- Being able to enjoy myself and especially keep enjoying myself!

11. FREEDOM

At the same time I understand that to me freedom is more than I'd just written down. It's also being able to let my dreams come alive. Thinking this, I start to wonder what it is I always have wanted to do.

When I close my eyes I go back to the days when I was just a little kid. I loved being able to think of new games and activities to entertain myself. I was always good at making up stuff and then have it come to life. Then I realize I've been missing out on this for a long time. I hardly do anything with it anymore. There's no creativity at work, no creativity in my spare time and at home it's also pretty boring. I know I'm not like that, I'm much more adventurous.

That same instant I vow to document this trip to the starts, once I get home. People may think it's a weird story, but I don't care. It's my story and if I get to inspire just one or two other people, I've already accomplished my goal. Next I start to look for some writing equipment in my bags.

To my surprise I find about everything, except for stuff to do with being creative. What has happened to all my pencils, markers and sketchbooks? There isn't one single marker or a sheet of paper. Nothing at all!

Attached to the suitcases are all these labels that literally represent burdens. They consist of tasks that other people have asked me to carry out for them. Some things relating to private stuff others involving work. I now wonder if these things are really that important to these other people. These labels also show short films of situations where I let the other people go before me, just to please them. I've never questioned what it is I would have liked to do, I only wondered about what it is the other person would have wanted.

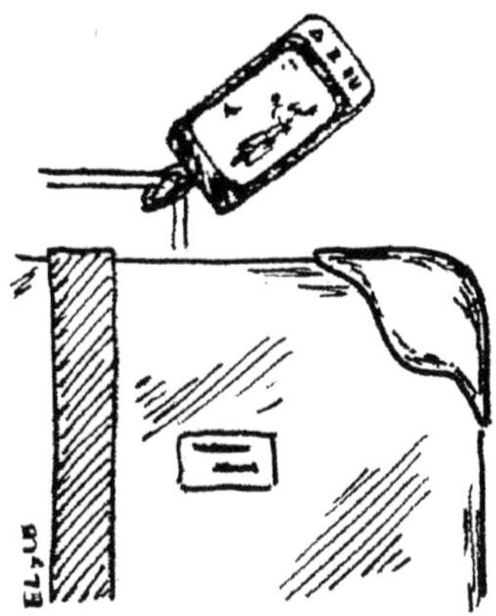

For some reason everyone around me has considered everything I've done up to now as normal. And the worst part is that if they had they done things themselves, instead of asking me, it would have cost them a lot less time and worries. Thus leaving me time to do things for myself that I've wanted to do for such a long time, like being creative.

From this moment on I decide I won't be picking up things for other people, simply because they ask me to. From now on I'll first ask whether I have any time or not and, if so, what would be needed to help this person out. If I want to consider helping others, I should have enough energy myself. I can only have enough energy if I start listening to myself and start doing fun (and important) things just for me!

12. THE WISHWAGON

I pull on the thick rope again and I can hear bells tingling all through the train. This time someone new appears, a lady called Sandy. It turns out she's the hostess of this train. She wants to know if everything is according to my wishes and if I might want something else. I'm completely caught of guard by this simple question. It's been such a long time since anyone has asked me what I would like to do! Sandy can tell I'm a bit confused and gives me a radiant smile.

Next, her eye catches my luggage filled with chores for other people and without any hesitation she picks up my luggage, puts in on a trolley, and hands over a wish coupon.

Sandy looks closely at me and then tells me that I can exchange this coupon for just about anything I need, in order to make the dream - I'd just been thinking about – come true. "Think wisely and carefully about what you are about to choose. This coupon is meant for you and for you only! You can get whatever it is you need, so you'll be able to finally start doing whatever it is you've always been longing to do. If it's your desire is to be more creative, then please do so! All this luggage you've just handed over gives you plenty of opportunity to start anew. You know, chances can be right there for the taking if you wish to see them. The less attention you pay them, the less visible they become. They are still there, but solely in the background. Not until we decide to act upon these chances, will they reappear loud and clear.

13. MY OWN PERSONAL TREASURE

After a short while Sandy returns to take me to another carriage. There's a plate on the door reading "Wish Wagon". "Try to think only about your wish when entering. Will you manage?" I nod my head, curious as to what might be in store for me. When entering the wagon I'm in for a big surprise. It's packed full of stuff for being creative. There are drawing supplies and art craft materials. There's also a laptop, packed with lots of suitable programs and applications.

I want something I can easily carry with me and which can be used for multiple purposes. I decide to go for a laptop. I look at Sandy to see if it's okay. She lets me know it's fine. She does give me a warning however. "Be sure not to use this laptop for others, 'because you'll be left without anything at all for yourself'. I take this warning to heart. Then Sandy gives me a sticker with a polestar on it. It's the same star that's on the treasure map and on top of the compass. The meaning starts to speak for itself. I put the sticker carefully on the top of the laptop. It now is really my laptop.

I get installed on the couch in my cabin with my new shiny laptop. It's looking amazing! When taking a closer look at it I see that an engraving has appeared in the top of the laptop. It's glowing and shining very gently, as if to tell me I'm on the right path. It feels like I am. It is as if I've just had a huge victory.

When opening up the laptop I begin to understand the true worth of this gift. It's packed with applications to make drawings and also other programs I can have a blast with. I can write pieces, create logos, and adjust sounds. Anything I can think of seems possible. What a wonderful gift this is!

At this moment I promise myself no one will ever be allowed to touch this laptop. This is my treasure and, being so, it's also the key to my future. That's remarkable. *The key to my future.* Could this really be the key? Or might this be the first key? While looking at the screen of the laptop a key appears on the right side. This is definitely one of the keys. I'm starting to understand lots of more keys are about to follow and I feel the excitement increasing in my system. This is becoming a wonderful adventure!

14. UNDERSTANDINGS

The first thing I decide to do is type in what I've just experienced. I'm writing down everything from the moment I woke up this morning (including dreaming about this journey), up to the moment that I got to burn my luggage and received this wonderful gift. It gets me thinking. What's the meaning of all of this? It seems logical, I'm just not sure yet what it is exactly.

Another thought comes to mind: How will I be dealing with people who want something from me, or better, who I allow to get something from me. Again it seems like I'm having a light bulb-moment. Other people asking me to do things for them and, as a result, taking up my time, is something I have let happen to me. It's not as if it's always been assumed by others that I would do just about anything for everyone. This has gradually developed in time. If I want to have some time left for myself, it's important to start changing things from now on.

I start to wonder what I can best do from now on. I do not have a clue. What to do right now? Maybe I should call Sandy?

15. A CONFRONTING DRAWING

Sandy must have heard me somehow, because the door opens and she sits down across from me.

Sandy looks me in the eye and asks me how I'm doing. She continues by asking: "What do you need in order to make your dream come true?" I do not know and I explain this to her. Can she help me find out? Sandy gives me a big smile and says: "But of course I can help you! That's what I'm here for." She opens a door in the wall behind the couch and grabs a large piece of paper. It's amazing to discover what's hidden in this train. Sandy puts the sheet down on the table and starts drawing. She then starts to talk.

She explains to me about this journey. At first she's drawing all my suitcases and bags on the right-hand side of the paper. Then she starts to draw me below this pile of luggage. I'm carrying this immense load on my shoulders. Oops, that's hard to look at. The way she's puts me down on paper I almost start to succumb beneath this load. I'm not trying to keep plates up in the air, which already is hard to do, no I'm carrying complete loads of baggage. Oh no, look… the plates… While one hand is holding the luggage, the other one is trying to keep those plates spinning. Then she starts to add words to every plate. The words are related to my work, my family and friends. Then Sandy adds more bags and suitcases on top of the plates I'm holding as to show the burden being the result of keeping everything running smoothly. Slowly I start to understand what she's sketching. All of these actions have immense impact on my life.

I'm starting to understand I want and need to change my life. From now on I want my freedom. I want freedom to do whatever it is I want to do. I want freedom of movement and also to have time for myself. I'm going to stop making promises to others, if they can do it just as easily themselves. If I can carry out my promises, it will cost me all the energy I have and as a result I won't have energy left for myself. That can't be right!

16. MASSIVE CLEAN-UP

"What do you think?" Sandy is looking at me with a huge smile. "How about throwing some of these plates out of the window? Would you like to?" She pulls out a bag from all the luggage and I can hear the sound of porcelain. I open up the bag and see all these plates with words written on them, just like the ones from the drawing. Sandy then opens the window and starts by throwing out one of the plates. Before I know it we are throwing out plates one after another. The more I throw away, the happier I become. I even start to yell from excitement!

At that same moment I hear rumbling going on behind and above me and just in time I can take a dive to keep me safe from all the bags and suitcases which are starting to fall down. The labels contain the same words that were written on the plates. I'm a bit startled. This is not what I had expected. By throwing away the plates I can no longer keep things up in the air and as a result everything came crashing down. It's amazing how everything comes to life in this train.

"Shall we go for a walk?" Sandy smiles at me and starts to pick up some of the suitcases while going out of the carriage. I begin to suspect what she might be up to and follow her, dragging along all of these suitcases and bags. It feels like I'm trying to move dead weight.

It's not easy but I manage to get the suitcases on the balcony of the train. I then notice we're riding above a ravine. This is the perfect moment to get rid off the entire luggage by throwing it overboard into the ravine, against the rocks, having them explode. I start to laugh just thinking about this prospect and while laughing my strength seems to increase.

I pick up the first suitcase and throw it overboard into the depth of the ravine. The suitcase crashes down on the rocks and turns into a huge explosion of fireworks. It's a wonderful spectacle to watch! At the same time I hear laughter and clapping behind me. Sandy and Marty are excited and are encouraging me to continue getting rid of these bags. Feeling this good about throwing down the first suitcase,

I decide to throw down some more into the ravine. I can hardly believe I had so much trouble carrying them around because of their weight, compared with how easy it is to simply throw them overboard. Each blast is bigger and better to watch. It's an amazing spectacle I'll keep remembering for a long time.

Then I hear the whistle getting blown. Henry is celebrating as well from the engine room. When the steam from the train merges with the clouds resulting from the explosion a wonderful drawing starts to appear. When I look closely I can see a key with directly below it the word "Freedom". It's true. This feeling of letting go adds to my feeling of freedom. How wonderful!!!

17. OVERVIEW

Enjoying the view, I'm aware I do not only have a marvellous view I can enjoy, but with the view comes overview.

Marty looks at me and then says to me: "Whenever you've had enough of something, you can always choose to return it or throw it out." Those words are absolutely true. If I no longer wish to do or hold on to something, I can always stop and give it back. Should I not be obligated to return it, I'm able to do with it whatever I think suitable. This also means that I no longer have to hold on to certain things. From now on I can make the choice to do, or not do, whatever it is I want to (not) do. Freedom!

Next, another loud noise can be heard and before I know it all these bags and suitcases start overflowing onto the balcony. A door of the carriage containing luggage has been opened and everything has landed with a huge crash on the tiny balcony of the train. We hardly are able to stand in this balcony ourselves, but what lot of fun we are having! Marty, Sandy and I are having so much fun! Apparently Henry has heard us laughing, because suddenly I hear the sound of the whistle from the steam train blowing as if it's joining us in our laughter!

I now feel invincible. This feels incredible! It's so nice to be on top of everything, while experiencing this feeling! One thing is for sure, whatever might happen, I will always remember this feeling!

Then Marty interrupts my thoughts. "What do you say? Do you want to go for another round of dumping luggage? I do however have something else to assist you if you want to. It's a small firecracker. If you put this in the middle of all these suitcases, it'll make all tracks disappear, as if there have never been any commitments you've made." This sounds okay to me and gratefully I accept the firecracker from Marty. I put it on top of a pile of suitcases. The firecracker now starts to ignite and before I know it all the luggage is gone. The only thing left is this trail of tiny, white flames, going throughout the entire carriage. Then a loud bang sounds. The wagon containing all luggage seems to explode. Startled I look at it and suddenly the carriage is shining. Not only is it shining, the carriage itself has been cleaned up. There is overview. There is only one thing left in the wagon. It's a key. Marty stretches his arm and the key comes flying into his hand.

Marty now offers me a new key. When I look at it closely, I discover it's not just a key, but it's actually an USB-stick I can use for my laptop, shaped like a key. Marty looks at me again and then says: "This is a form of luggage that not only weights less, but also is more flexible. Whenever you have had enough of something, you can decide to "delete" it. This saves you a lot of extra baggage and noise!" Having said this, he puts the USB-key in my hand with a huge smile.

18. PARTY TIME!

Sandy wraps her arm around me. "Congratulations! You now are one step closer to your own dreams and desires! It's party time!!!"

We go back inside the train, into another carriage. This one turns out to be a Party Wagon. It's so amazing to find out what's present in this train. First there was a Wish Wagon, now there is a Party Wagon. Apparently something can appear to come out of nowhere, if you know where to look for it and how to get there!

The moment we want to enter the Party Wagon, the train starts to shake uncontrollably. When I look out of the window, I'm completely surprised. I can see the train lifting from the tracks. We are flying up in the air! With all the baggage gone, the train finally can get up to speed, since we now are no longer bound by gravity. Nothing can pull us down anymore. We are free!!! This is such a great feeling. I cry from excitement and listen to Henry blowing the whistle of the steam train a few more times.

"Vreeeeeeeeeeeew vreeeeeeeeeeeew". It's the best sound I've ever heard. It's been a long time since I've been so absolutely happy and ecstatic!

The Party Wagon has been decorated with balloons and garlands. It's looking cosy. To make things a bit more festive, I'm being offered a glass of sparkling wine. The bubbly makes me a bit lightheaded and also more cheerful. Slowly the world is starting to spin and it's like the carriage is changing. Didn't this used to be the wagon in which the luggage exploded? Straight away the carriage starts to change again. There now is a starry sky visible with in between keys.

19. A WAGON FILLED WITH INSPIRATION

When looking at the ceiling of the carriage, I not only see the starry sky, but I also see words lighting up next to the stars. There are beautiful words visible such as “trust”, “freedom”, “fortitude” and “perseverance”. Another corner of the wagon shows words linked to creativity, including “inspiration” and “communication”, but also “resourcefulness”.

I’m a bit surprised about the word “communication”. Then Sandy is standing next to me. She explains to me: “Creativity is the result of inspiration from the world around us. Just look at the stars and planets for instance, like the sun and the moon. How many stories have been written around these heavenly bodies? Think about the “man in the moon” or “the stars in the sky representing our beloved ones who’ve passed away”.

“Since last night you’ve dreamt about a number of keys. You’ve seen those keys and even received some of them. These keys represent specific thoughts. These thoughts are the result of inspiration and lead to both creativity and resourcefulness. The keys also represent solution and make it possible to find certain answers.”

“In the past people assumed the earth was flat and the sun revolved around the earth. It took centuries before it was known that the earth was round and was circling around the sun. The idea of looking at the earth from a different perspective, was perceived from a thought or feeling coexisting between universe and men. The receiver experienced some sort of "flow". That's why there's this expression about "experiencing a flow". This is about being inspired and as a result becoming creative and inventive, thus resulting in discoveries and leading to new creations."

"This flow of events has led to you being on this steam train, as well as you having various views and ideas. One could say your desire to be creative has received a new boost today. You know, communication is a very subtle process. When you're in tune with receiving those subtle signals, you'll notice numerous ideas and thoughts can enter your mind, you never have thought about before. Because you're now open to this never ending stream of thought, it gets proven time and time again that the unachievable all of a sudden has become achievable."

"As human beings we're excellent at blocking signals simply by being occupied with our day to day business that we must do every day. But who has told us we need to do so and who are we doing this for? Today is the day you get to think about what it is you would truly like to do. And to assist you in this process, various words are being shown on the ceiling of this carriage."

"Do you see any words you could to use? Maybe there are certain values or features which are useful?" I answer: "I'd like to remain more focused. I have the tendency to follow others instead of sticking to my own decision." "Determination perhaps?" Sandy asks. "Sounds good", I respond. In the corner of the carriage a star begins to shine.

Sandy asks me to extend my arm and next thing I know, the star starts to move. If floats from the ceiling towards me and lands in my hand. How remarkable! Anything is possible if you're open to it! If there's anything I'm learning from this adventure, it's that things can change!

Sandy interrupts my thoughts. “Indeed anything is possible. The question however is do you get influenced by the circumstances or do you stay true to your original plan? This is an excellent souvenir for you. Just look at what is says!” The star reads “determination”. Very appropriate. Sandy then continues: “Take this star with you and put it in your treasure chest. This way you can always hold on to the targets you’ve set, even when everything seems to hold you down. This star will help you remember that you can achieve anything you set your mind to!” Sandy gives me a big smile and then leaves the carriage.

20. TRUST

Back alone again, lots of thoughts are running through my mind. I'm thinking about the story related to determination, about the realisation that anything is possible if you do not get scared off by circumstances and about the treasure chest.

How would Sandy know about the chest? Why wouldn't she? She seems to know just about anything! What did she mean when she started talking about remembering?

Then Sandy is back again. She seems to be able to read my mind. "People are experts when it comes to making resolutions. Just look at the New Year. We all seem to be making resolutions. Stories are being written about this topic and also people are asking one another about these resolutions. The simple fact that people are do this year after year, says quite a lot. It shows that people like to get tempted or persuaded to make changes in their lives. Being able to hold on to these resolutions is quite a different thing though. How many really live up to these resolutions? And if people do live up to these resolutions for how long do they do so? There always seems to be an excuse for letting go of these intentions. Old habits die hard and it's easier to rely on these past habits then to stick firmly to newly made resolutions. That's why it's good to have a reminder every now and then. This will help you to hold on to your intention instead of falling back because of circumstances or laziness."

I'm listening with fascination to what she's telling me. Then she continues. "Have you ever wondered why you are getting all these keys?" No, I had not. Not yet anyway. "Those keys will help you to reveal the information you need in order to reach those dreams and desires. This includes all characteristics and necessities.

What else do you need?" Suddenly the word TRUST comes to mind. Trust to believe that whatever it is I'm doing is good enough. Trust to believe it's possible to do things in a different way. Trust to accept that what I'm experiencing really is true. Sandy is looking at me as if she's reading my thoughts. She seems to be happy with everything I'm thinking about right now. She gives me an answer: "Trust is a beautiful and also remarkable word. However “trust” is not something to be taken lightly. It’s something delicate. It can be very supportive, but when experiencing lack of support, the World can seem like a dark place to be and dark places can be hard to live in. Trust can help you to stay true to yourself when others are trying to distract you or are failing in showing you any support. Considering all of this, the question is “what’s going to help you maintain your trust?” Again the word “trust” is an excellent choice, but it takes more courage, support and explanation to yourself compared to a word like “determination”. ”

“Now hold out your hand to receive this quality. When you unfold your treasure map, you’ll see you’ll be able to put both stars on top of the stars drawn on the fabric. Just go do it!” I grab both stars and lay them on top of the drawn stars. Right away they become one with the shapes on the map. The words seem to be embroidered in the stars. With every word and every quality this treasure map seems to be coming more to life.

Next, the two of us go outside, leaving the carriage. When I’m on the balcony I notice it’s already dark outside. The stars seem to be getting closer and closer, but it will take a while before we’ll get there. Sandy now interrupts my thoughts. “We still have some work to do! Will you escort me to your carriage?” I nod and then follow her back inside.

21. THE DREAM DESIGNER

When I arrive at the wagon the drawing is still lying on the table. Things seem to have been changed. Suitcases have vanished and I now have been drawn as a person who's standing powerfully and firmly. It's someone who's determined to do what feels right and who has confidence in everything that's about to happen. It also seems like a person who wants freedom and also likes to investigate numerous things. The word I'm starting to think about is CREATIVITY. By investigating, new ideas can arise, which are important motivators for being creative.

Sandy draws a magnifying glass and binoculars on the sheet of paper. When I'm looking through the magnifying glass the world seems to be completely different. Next Sandy's drawing a telescope. It's very special and helps bringing the stars really close. Then a younger version of me starts to run across the paper. This version of me is very curious and gets very excited when seeing the telescope.

The young version of me is ready to be an investigator. All information is being absorbed by me and makes me feel happy. Then the younger me starts to draw really quickly. Complete models arise on the drawing paper. I never knew I could be this creative! When Sandy has finished sketching I'm looking at a dream I used to have back in the days. It was a dream to become a "designer". Not just a designer, but a designer who's helping other people to investigate their dreams and making them a reality. It's like being a "dream designer".

Sandy then explains what's going on: "Every dream starts by deciding to become true to you. When you do not prioritize yourself, you forget what's truly important to you. Because of this journey you are starting to remember who you are and what it is you like and what you've always wanted to do, even when you were still a small child. You like to help people based on your creativity. Your passion is to help people to return to their origin. From this point they can act from freedom."

I need some time to think about this. Wow, have I ever thought about this or said so? But then I see the younger version of me talking to other people. I'm comforting other people, sitting next to them and listening to them. Next I get my magic wand and have their wishes appear magically from my hat.

Vaguely I remember having a magic kit, including wand and magic hat. My wish back then was to help other people's wishes come true. Even when I was a small kid, I first thought of others, before thinking about myself. This felt natural to me. If other people were happy, so was I. By bringing wishes from other people to life and having their wishes come true, I was able to be creative myself.

When looking at the big drawing paper I see new words existing. It's a sort of saying: "Creating creativity from creativity." I translate this for myself to: "Creating something new for someone from inspiration." Well, that's most certainly like magic, isn't it? It's just as wonderful and true as "Creating miracles by dreaming miracles".

Could it really be this simple? Sandy answers: "We as people have the tendency to make everything as hard as possible. It's easier to say something is impossible, than to investigate it. That's why a lot of people are not motivated at all. It's like with those New Year's resolutions. To be able to execute those, change is needed. And those changes, that's what people most of the time see as unachievable. That's why having faith is so important!"

It's like everything now has come full circle. "Having faith, trusting repeatedly, eventually leads to freedom". I repeat this to myself. "Trust leads to freedom". It leads to inner freedom but also to freedom in daily life.

I'm pleasantly surprised there's all this inspiration on this train. It seems like all answers just pop up in my head. If only I can manage to keep this state of mind when getting home..." At that moment I feel the training slowing down and coming to a halt.

22. THE KEY

We are standing still amidst the stars. To my right I can see a flickering key. It seems to be calling out to me. Marty is standing right behind me and he tells me I can pick my key now. He adds: “Please note that we won’t be waiting forever, so you might want to rush a little”.

I stretch my arm and grab the key from the sky. There’s a sentence on the side of the key: “Trust leads to freedom”. That’s amazing, I just though about that! When I turn the key around I see another phrase: “Creativity creates creativity”. I now become aware these are my own thoughts, inscribed into the key. This is my personal key!

Marty then adds: “It’s more than just your key. This is the key that will help you achieve your dreams. So please look after this key very well!” I wrap my key in a towel and sit down again on the couch. I’m becoming aware of this happy feeling inside of me. It’s the felling that I can accomplish anything I want to, if only I dare to dream and also dare to trust.

All of a sudden I’m dozing off. Before I get to realize I’ve already fallen asleep. The whole trip back home is something I have no knowledge of.

23. THE STATION, A BIT DIFFERENTLY…

It's already light outside when I wake up. I can hear the sound of the birds and the crickets, combined with the sound of a puffing steam train slowing down. The train comes to a halt at the station. When I left the station it was an abandoned and quiet building, but now it's full of life. I see scenes I never could have imagined. Animals are walking inside and outside of the building. Flowers and trees are blooming everywhere. It seems like a paradise but on a tiny scale. Or maybe it's actually real size. I've never seen anything like this.

Then Henry is standing next to me. "Just take a look at all your luggage. It's reduced to hardly anything. You only have a small bag left. You can be very proud of yourself. Everything that was redundant, has been either tossed away by your or been burnt. All that you're carrying at this instant is what matters to you. Look at that small bundle that's left. I see my backpack with in it a large rolled-up drawing, my laptop, an USB-stick shaped like a key, my canvas treasure map and a handful of stars and keys. In my pocket I can feel the compass, glowing gently.

"You might want to hurry back to the beach. There you will find a chest you can use to stash all your belongings. You can then take it home and think about everything that has happened these past 24 hours." I'm looking at Henry and I feel the tears rolling from my eyes. This was such an amazing trip. Deep down, I do not want to leave at all. Then I hear Marty's voice. He's showing me two tickets." Here you are. Here are two tickets. One is for you if you decide to go on another journey with us. The other one is for someone you might think is up to a trip like this. We expect to see you again in the future!"

I take the tickets and very cautiously I put them in my backpack. The tickers have the colour of sand and are marked with stars. These tickets are still brand new however. I look at Sandy, Marty and then Henry. “Thank you so much. This was a very special event!” I give each of them a hug and when it’s Henry’s turn he looks me in the eye with a big smile. “What do you think? Care to blow the whistle yourself?”

I join Henry and see everybody boarding the train. When I blow the whistle, steam starts to arise from everywhere and the train now goes up in smoke. I blink my eyes and the train has gone. In the back of my mind I can hear Marty, Henry and Sandy’s voices. They are wishing me good luck, lots of fun and especially lots of freedom, trust and creativity. I shake my head in disbelief and next thing I know I’m back on the beach.

24. THE CHEST

I'm standing near the flood mark once again and I'm witnessing the pile of sand. Something stands out. This time it's like the corner of a chest. I wipe the sand away and out comes this beautiful chest with the most amazing woodcarving. The person who made this, must not only have had a creative mind, but also been very handy. Or maybe this person still is. It's an absolute piece of craftsmanship.

I'm smiling thinking that I can be as capable in whatever I wish to be doing if only I take the time to do so. I'm getting completely happy once more. If only I have trust and keep the faith, I can achieve anything I want to!

The chest has been locked. Somehow, this lock seems to be familiar to me. I get the distinct impression one of my keys could fit. The first key already is a perfect match. The chest opens up and turns out to be divided in many compartments, which are shaped like stars and keys. Way in the back of a corner is a tubular case. It's perfect for my drawings, even though it might be a bit small. I take a look at the drawing in my backpack. Where is it? It was so big, it didn't fit my backpack and it was sticking out. When looking more closely, I see how this large sheet of paper has transformed into a small object, decorated with a ribbon. It fits the tubular case perfectly. Lastly I see there's one compartment left. It's shaped like a compass. Carefully I put the compass in. I can't help but smile. Someone has made this perfectly!

I put the chest in my backpack close to the laptop. When I take a look at the time on my watch I'm surprised to see it's one o' clock in the afternoon. Exactly 24 hours have passed since I came here and found the treasure map. A piece of newspaper flies by, carried by the wind and falls down before my feet. I pick it up and read the article. "Tonight for the second time in a row a clear starry sky was visible and keys have been sighted yet again. Just like last night, no keys have been recorded on film."

Next my eye is caught by a small ad. It's surrounded by starts and in the middle is a keyhole. There are some lines of text next to it stating: "You have just experienced your first journey to the stars. You have found the keys to help you accomplish your dreams. I you wish to realize new dreams, please show up at the nearest beach at one o'clock in the afternoon. There you'll find new instructions to bring you to our meeting point "Station to the Stars".

Looking once more the article has vanished. I'm back at my kitchen table, holding the newspaper. Next to me is a perfectly shaped and manufactured treasure chest…

PART TWO

Notification

1. INTRODUCTION

In this part of the book, the story from part one will be looked at more closely. There will be an explanation on how our brain works, followed by the meaning of each chapter and how you can apply this yourself. We can distinguish the following composition which influences how we feel, think and as a result act:

False Securities
We'll start with False Securities. This is about living your life according a regular structure, without wondering if this really is what you want your life to be like. You are used to the rhythm of the train and being told by others what you should and shouldn't be doing. The train has a fixed route and all you have to do is get in on time and get off at the expected stop and time, invented by others.

Trigger
There might come a moment in life where you may start to think about what it is you really want to do. This can be a short period of time, or a longer one, depending on what you think is achievable. A "trigger" has caused you to think about this, being the result of an event that has touched a certain sensitive area deep within.

Mindsets or survival mechanisms
If and when you respond to so called "triggers" has everything to do with your "mindset". Do you think you can change? Is there any reason for you to even think about changing?

Mindsets started to exist at an age you weren't able to understand the world, let alone create an overview. As a result the mindset created isn't based on logic, but on emotions. This mindset has been stored in the subconscious part of the brain that is based on these emotions instead of logic. Since it's not stored in the conscious part of the brain, it's hard to get access to it, especially because most of the time you're not aware that any such mindsets even exists.

Dreams
Whenever you start to become aware of having mindsets, you can start to explore those and decide whether to change them. Change

requires motivation though. A proper motivation can arise from dreams. Dreaming is something you do when you're asleep, but also is optional during the day. The dreams during the day can be consciously created and even awakened. Those dreams will help you remember what it is you've always (or since recently) wanted to do.

Rationality ⇔ Feelings
Whether a dream is a nice dream or not, is recognised by the feeling it leaves you with. Dreams are connected to your intuition and as such to your feelings. During the day however we work with rationality. Everything must be made out and especially be verified. But what if we were to limit ourselves when doing so? What if there are possibilities as huge as we dare to dream? Would you dare to withstand this feeling of insecurity and follow your dreams? Or would you stick to the rational part inside of you, telling you things can't be changed easily and therefore you need to stay in line with what you've always done.

Signals
Whenever you've decided that changing might an option, you can start to change certain beliefs and with these your mindsets. You may know what it is you want to do and how you're feeling, but it's also important to learn to recognise the signals, guiding you towards your goal.

Changing your mindset
When you have set your goal(s), are able to recognise the signals and dare to follow up on your feelings and intuition, you're ready to start changing your mindsets. This starts by trying to find out and understand what may have happened in the past, which has led to a specific pattern of behaviour. You can also simply focus on what it is you want to do or to achieve. The mindsets you want to create are meant to help you out to achieve your new goal(s).

Qualities
To be certain that your new mindset(s) are working properly and being used to their full capacity, it's important to find out whether or not you are missing certain qualities needed to succeed. You also might want to consider whether you have habits or qualities that

might work against you. By becoming aware of your new mindset you can start to embrace (new) skills or let go of certain habits.

Anchoring your mindset

Once you've decided to change your mindset and set a new one, it's important to anchor this new mindset. This way you'll be prevented from being pulled back into your old false securities and habits. You can do so by anchoring your newly founded mindset.

Storage of the brains

When you start to anchor your mindset, you make it optional to recall your mindset. It's no longer hidden in the subconscious part of your brain; it's anchored in the conscious part of the brain. As a result you can use both your feelings as well as your rationality to call upon your mindset.

New adventures

When you're able to use your rationality, in order to check your new beliefs, you can adjust those beliefs and corresponding mindsets whenever you feel like it or whenever you need to. From now on you can achieve anything you want and whatever feels okay to you. You now know how to act and as a result choose how you want to live and lead your life. Here's to new adventures! Cheers!

2. FALSE SECURITIES

Explanation:
Many people live their lives according to a steady routine. Day after day they do the same thing; from getting up in the morning, 'till they go to bed. Once, living according to such a tight schedule might have been a challenge. So ask yourself, do you have a routine, purely out of old habits? Can you do without the routine? Is this routine living you instead of the other way around? Or can it be that other people are forcing you into this daily routine?

Many people believe that if they live according to what they're used to when it comes to getting up in time for work and keeping to agreements, their jobs will always be secure. Is a job secure, simply because you are doing the same routing and/or what you are expected to do? In the current time of technology and reorganisations, the only stability we have is that things are going to change at some given moment. Unfortunately everyone is supposed to change accordingly.

In this book:
The main character in this book does a lot of things for other people. This makes our character feel as if they are doing something useful. The question however is if this assumption is true. Do people really appreciate their effort? If so, does our character feel happy doing so? What used to feel like being useful and helpful may now very well feel like carrying a very heavy burden. The security it may once have offered might have changed over time into a lack of support.

Questions:

- Do you get into the train because others expect you to and then have yourself transported to a certain location to get off on a certain time? If so, what's your purpose in doing so?

3. TRIGGERS

Explanation:
A large number of people like living according to this steady routine we just discussed. It gives them peace of mind. It also gives them a sense of security, because they know what to expect. What happens when this routine gets interrupted? Or better yet: what if the routine would stay the same forever? Would someone ever get bored? Would you get bored and wonder if there would be something else in this life? Do you want to grow old living in such a way?

Triggers help you to break out of a pattern. Triggers can come from inside yourself, causing you to feel the need for change. They can also be the result of something happening around you and as a result being decided for you. Your situation might be changing and you do not have any option but to go along with it. How this change will effect you is up to you though. Will you go along with what's being asked or do you decide to take control yourself?

When a trigger comes from inside, a certain wish starts to arise. You can feel it because you may feel uneasy at times. This uneasiness can be the result of talking to other people, having dreams or by things happening around you. Think about people who suddenly pass away, decide to emigrate or are given a wonderful promotion.

In this book:
In this book there are a number of examples:

- The dream about the journey to the stars;
- The first article in the newspaper;
- The labels attached to the suitcases triggering memories;
- The confrontational drawing having our main character hold on to luggage, while keeping the plates spinning high up in the air;
- The train speed.

The dream helps our main character to think about new possibilities. By reading the article the person starts to move. Our character had no idea things would start to change because of this trip. Changes were accomplished by receiving assignments to do with the luggage:

- What luggage will you be taking with you? What will you be leaving behind?
- What suitcases or bags can you get rid off so the train can increase speed?

Next, our character received useful information when the drawing was made. It resulted in a confrontational insight and with that it gave the person a glimpse of reality. Only when our character witnessed their life, were they able to think about whether this was a comfortable life or not. The answer came rather quickly. This was not the most optimal, wished-for situation.

Questions:

- What do you do when things start to change in your surroundings? Will you go along with what's been asked or do you decide to act upon it?
  Please note, that the decision to go along can be an excellent choice, if and when this choice has been made by you!
- Do you like it when everything stays the same for a longer period of time? Do you get a bit restless every now and then when nothing special happens? Do you dare to give in to this internal feeling of restlessness?
- Do you feel change is optional?

4. SURVIVAL MECHANISMS

Explanation:
Whether you will respond to triggers by undertaking concrete actions has everything to do with your mindset. Do you feel it's an option to change? Or won't you even make the slightest attempt, because you don't think it will ever happen?

Mindsets have originated at a young age when you weren't able to rationalize things in a logical manner. As a result a mindset or survival mechanism has been created which can't be accessed in that same logical manner, because it has been stored in the unconscious part of the brain. Therefore you won't have any recollection of it when growing up.

Our brains start to develop when we are still in the womb. While growing up, connections are made, we learn to recognise and respond to impulses and at some moment we learn to interpret certain events. It takes until about 7 years of age before we are able to understand and categorise events and put things in perspective. Once we start going to school this process starts to evolve.

Our first impressions and experiences are taking place well before the age of 7 years old. As a result, we react based on primal instinct, since we cannot apply any logic at that age. This (primary) reaction is now linked to an emotion, consistent with what we experienced at that moment. As a result, any time a similar event happens, this emotion can surface and this primary reaction is (re)activated. Even when we're older, we'll still be reacting based on this first experience.

When we start to get older (and wiser) we start to become aware that these mindsets or survival mechanisms do not support us any longer. We would like to get rid off these mechanisms. The strategy we apply time and again was based on the amount (or better yet lack) of logic we had when this mindset was created. It hasn't improved when developing our other skills and knowledge and as a result it's holding us back. You might start to have certain dreams and wish to change things, but in practice this isn't an option, since each time you try you seem to be held back by yourself.

In this book:
A number of situations are mentioned in this book that create and sustain certain mindsets:

In the book, a number of situations are presented:

- Playing in the sandpit;
- The train at the schoolyard.

When our main character is playing in the sandpit, their game gets cruelly interrupted by the presence of other children wanting to play as well. These kids are probably not aware that they are interrupting, but in fact they do. Next, they take away the toys, so they can play with them. Our main character then is carried inside for protection. The lesson our character has learned is that when others arrive, they can do just about anything. They do not get punished for their actions; it's our character that has to endure being carried inside, while the sun is shining outside.

The same thing happens while wanting to play inside the train at the schoolyard. When our main character finally gets the chance to ride the train, they must go inside again.

Questions:

- Are you convinced there are certain things you will never be able to achieve?
- Is it possible you think this to be impossible because something seems to be holding you back?
- Might it be possible that whatever is holding you back, could be caused by something you have experienced in the past? If so, are those thoughts really true?

5. DREAMS

Explanation:
As a child we had numerous dreams and wishes about what it is we wanted to be. Some of us wanted to become vets, others dancers, some of us artist.

When reaching a certain grade at school, a time comes to think about choosing a direction fitting you future choice of profession. Does this direction match the dreams you used to have (or maybe still have), or are you going to choose a "safe" choice, which will ensure you of work, the possibility to keep developing or making a lot of money.

When we finally have a job, the question is if this is what we always desired to be or to do, or have we started to work somewhere purely coincidental and as a result have developed in a similar coincidental direction.

Many people start wondering some day whether this is it. This question most often has to do with dreams. When there is little or no chance for change, improvements or developing, does one still want to continue this lifestyle or line of work? In the early days one might have called this a "midlife crisis", but nowadays this phenomena is already visible around the age of 30. It is no longer considered "normal" to work your entire life for one company and as a result the question "what now?" presents itself much sooner in life than it used to do. Combined with everything going at an enormous speed nowadays, things constantly changing, us being considered to do multiple things at the same time, it's understandable that we experience this restlessness during our lives, leading to certain desires.

In this book:
In this book a number of dreams are discussed:

- Journey to the stars;
- Dream of the dream designer.

Dreams can happen during the night, but we can also have dreams during the day. The dream about travelling to the start was during the night-time, while our main character was asleep. This dream explained that things could change.

The dream of the dream designer was far more concrete. Our main character literally could observe what they always had wanted to do, in this case “designing”. Sometimes we need someone to take us by the hand and to experience what it is we really always wanted to do. In this book our character is being supported by the hostess, Sandy.

Questions:

- Is there something you’ve always dreamt about? If so, what is it?
- Have you recently thought of something you really would like to do?
- What is it you did not do or let pass you by, because it seemed more logical to choose a different path?

6. RATIONALITY ⇔ FEELINGS

Explanation:
Our brain can be divided in different sections. Most of us have heard about the division between the left part of the brain and the right side of the brain. The left side is most of the time our dominant side and as such determines our rationality. The right side of the brain then represents our submissive side and represents feelings.

We are used to trust our logic, since it's far easily accessible and we are trained to use it from an early age on at school. As a result using our intuition is something we rarely do. Whether using our rationality really works more efficiently (as we are taught to believe) is debatable. If you examine everything in detail, it will consume a lot of time in comparison to using your intuition, which can lead to a decision in a split second. If you are using your intuition it does require, however, that you know how to trust your intuition. This can only be achieved by exercising and working your intuition and frequently using your feelings.

In this book:
In the book there are a number of examples regarding using intuition:

- Trusting the glowing of the compass;
- Becoming aware of the weight of the luggage and how uneasy this was feeling.

At the moment the compass started to glow, the main character decided to follow the direction being lead by the compass. There wasn't any logical basis for doing so; it was a hunch being followed.

When the drawing was being sketched, our main character became aware of the weight of the luggage that was present and, as result, wanted not to be living a life that was ruled by someone else anymore. Because of this realisation, our main character started to wonder whether the other person appreciated and could really use their help, as they presumed originally. This feeling led to giving the rationality new impulses.

Questions:

- How often do you (dare to) trust your feelings?
- Has it ever occurred that you decided to go for logic, instead of your feelings, when in fact your intuition was proven to be right?
- How would it be to use your feelings as input for any actions?

7. SIGNALS

Explanation:
When using your feelings at regular intervals, certain signals will start to become recognisable. When something feels right, mostly it feels nice and comfortable. When something is wrong, it mostly feels heavy or uneasy.

There are a number of ways possible to learn how to live with your intuition and feelings. The first one is the result of experiencing a strong emotion, for instance as a result of an accident or when being really scared by an event or person. Secondly you can think about something you really like to do, like going on a vacation. Thirdly you can give your brain a job to do. All of these scenarios result in moving the conscious part of the brain (rationality) to the background. Next, the subconscious part, being the creative part and representing emotions and feelings, can start to manifest itself. Now any hidden memories, desires and feelings can come to the surface.

Whenever you are in a different state of mind than usual, like being very relaxed or alert and focused, your perception is different compared to usual. You can see and hear things your normally would miss out on, which can be compared with the difference between driving yourself or being on the passenger side. Because your perception is different from normal, you'll remember the event in a different way than normal and you can start to pick up signals you normally wouldn't notice.

Signals can help you understand if you are on the right or on the wrong path. It's important to learn how to recognise those signals. Sometimes they can be very obvious, like a red stoplight. Sometimes it's necessary to learn to see and recognise those signals.

In this book:

During the trip our main character becomes aware of things they never had seen before like:

- The station;
- The stars;
- The keys.

When our main character wakes up there's one sign after another. Starting with newspaper clippings including messages and then there turned out to be a station. There is also a compass giving clues and then there are words in the carriage, including matching stars and again signs.

Some of these signs only show for a second (like the article in the paper) and others remain for a long time (like the compass). Being guided by these signals our main character now experiences a whole new adventure. If our character had not followed up on these instructions in the article, this day would have been a day like every other day. Now however there was a possibility to experience something new and get new insight information.

Questions:

- Have you ever decided to change your decision based on a (swift) signal?
- Have you every seen things and wondered why you got to see them at that exact moment?
- Have you ever let yourself be guided by these signals? What did this feel like? Was this disappointing for you or did it result in new experiences?

8. CHANGING YOUR MINDSET

Explanation:
When you feel agitated a lot and you decide you would like to change this, the time is right to start changing your mindset. If you want to change your mindset it's important to ask yourself:

- What bothers you (most);
- What is it you would like to change?

The moment you make the decision to start doing certain things in a different way and to act accordingly, you've already started changing your mindset. You now start to understand your old mindset no longer works optimally for you (if working at all) and as a result you can determine how you want to respond. When you think about what you want to do exactly, you can keep adjusting what it is you want to achieve, until it feels okay.

In this book:
In this book our main character has decided to no longer put others ahead of themselves. By doing so in the past the main character didn't have any time to do things they wanted to do. No longer did they have any time to do fun things. Our main character also concluded they wanted to be more creative and assist others finding out what they would like to do. Our main character would still be helping them, but in a different, more assisting manner.

Questions:

- What convictions do you have that you want to maintain?
- What would you like differently?
- What would you like to get rid off completely?

9. QUALITIES

Explanation:
Deciding that you want to change things is one thing. It's something else to decide what skills you need (or want to adjust) to help support your conviction.

A lot of people can tell what it is they do NOT want anymore, but most of the time they fail at listing to what it is they do want. When you do not know what you want, try saying: "I NO longer want to… I DO however want to… By saying this out loud answers can arise to the surface, opposed to randomly making up a number of things you would like to do,

In this book:
Our main character would like to change a number of things:

- Checking out the amount of energy and time they have after doing things for themselves, instead of letting others go first;
- Two important qualities are mentioned:
  - Determination;
  - Trust.

  Both qualities are needed to stay true to oneself and assuming things will be alright again.

Questions:
- What qualities would you like to hold on to?
- What qualities are sabotaging you? Could you rephrase those positively?
- What qualities need working on? What would they be like when working best?

10. ANCHORING YOUR MINDSET

Explanation:
It now is important to hold on to your new goals and your new matching mindset(s). It is important to avoid being pulled back into false securities. This can be achieved by anchoring your new mindsets, this new survival mechanism.

By knowing what it is you want and which qualities you'll need, you can start by applying your new mindset. The most important question is if you can persevere in doing so for at least three months. As human beings we are used to falling back into our old patterns if we do not manage to hold on to our new beliefs right away. That's why it's so important to keep remembering the feelings and emotions that match your new goal, when executing this new mindset.

Feel what is happening to you when you are thinking about your mindset being executed and as a result your goal is being reached. Now hook this up to a matching thought or gesture.

Each time you feel the need to get back to your old habits, you can recall your new mechanism by applying that gesture or thinking about that thought. By doing so again and again, this new mechanism will become easier and easier to execute.

There is also another method to change and anchor your mindset. You then go back to the original event that caused this mindset. By expressing what's on your mind, you can empower yourself. By repeating these words in the (near) future, you can prevent yourself from executing your old mindset when being in a similar situation. Instead you can respond in the way you feel appropriate.

In this book:
Our main character has several methods, helping to hold on to the newly made resolution. By studying these or thinking about them, they have a clear reminder of how to act according to the new mindset.

Our main character has received a number of keys with lines on them. There are also a number of stars inscribed with words. When reading those lines or words, it's easier to apply the new strategy.

Questions:

- What symbols could be useful to you? Will you succeed by just making up a resolution or do you need to write it down and/or maybe read it back?
- Which methods will help you to remind you of your intention? What would be appropriate for you and also executable?

11. STORAGE OF THE BRAINS

Explanation:
In this second part of the book we've discussed some of the things which are going on in the brain. Our brains are using one part that can be accessed directly (the conscious part) and another part that's far less accessible (the unconscious part).

The part we are not (or less) aware of contains a lot of information that seems to be stored randomly. It's linked to numerous events, senses and/or emotions. It's important to be aware of the consequences of this kind of storage in the brain (setting a mindset unconsciously), so we can decide to stop using this kind of information and replace it by information that's usable (changing our mindset consciously).

When we use reference points, we can recall information that's normally hard to access, relatively easily. The reference point is like a key accessing the unconscious part of the brain, which stores your survival mechanisms. The anchoring process uses emotions and feelings present. This has been linked to a certain symbol that's easily remembered. When you start to become aware of a certain emotion, the thought of changing this can now arise. When you do not remember how, just use the symbol, which will help you reconnect with your previous intentions. This way you can recollect what it is you want, how you'd like it and how to execute this. The realisation you can actually accomplish this now will return.

By understanding this process we no longer have to respond to mindsets hidden in the unconscious part of our brain, instead we can react the way we would like to. Our brains are not aware these events have not happened for real, but only in our mind. They do however link emotions and feeling to certain thoughts and events. This way we can connect to very powerful mechanisms (new mindsets), we've programmed consciously in the unconscious part of the mind.

In this book:
When we check out the comparisons from the storage in our subconscious to our book, we can compare this to the suitcases. Unwillingly and unknowingly we are dragging along lots of luggage. Becoming aware of this luggage is the first step.

The second step consists of recollecting this luggage, specifically the content. As long as the suitcases are stored away safely, there's no need to think about them or even clean it up. The trouble with hidden memories is they have a tendency to show up when you do not want them. By making the decision to go on a journey, the suitcases become visible. It appears there are a large number of these bags and it's hard to keep an overview, if not impossible.

This takes us to the third step. What to do with the contents of our luggage? Do we know how we can use it? Is it indeed usable or is it time to change this content? In this book the luggage has been divided in usability. Everything which can no longer be used, gets burned, thrown away and gets removed. The content that is usable however, will be replaced by a USB stick. The stick is easily accessible by means of laptop. All other information can be found by studying the drawings.

This leads us to step four, getting the information structured and organized. The information is no longer to be found in several places, but is stored on the stick. All programs needed, can be found on the laptop. The drawings can be stashed in a tube, which can be stored in a tiny corner of the chest or be unfolded, so everything can be studied in an organised manner.

Lastly there's a key available, which helps finding back the information more easily and makes it possible to use this information and intentions in a far more accessible manner.

Questions:

- Can you remember what you did this morning?
- When was the last time you were angry? What did you do at that moment?
- How would it be to remember something amazing permanently, instead of letting it slip by?

12. NEW ADVENTURES

Explanation:
You now have learnt to apply your logic to anything you want to accomplish. As a result you can also check your progress with your new plans. You can check your mindsets and beliefs and, if needed, you can have them adjusted.

When you think on a regular basis about all the things you've intended to do and how far along your plans are, you'll become far more aware of your intentions. Next, you can check what's gone right and what's gone wrong. In both cases, go check to see what's happened to your survival mechanisms. Did you use those? Did they help? Do they need some more adjustments?

Each time you'll be experiencing certain emotions, telling you you're being held back, you can now start to use the methods explained in the previous chapters of part two of this book.

In this book:
Our main character receives two tickets after the journey is over. They are meant to inspire others and also to return if needed. All our character has to do is return to the beach and a new journey will begin. This new journey will then help to become aware of other mindsets and help to formulate new strategies.

Questions:

- Are you up for a new mindset? What do you need to go on an adventure yourself?

Finally:
You now know you can achieve anything you want! Now go do it!!!

ACKNOWLEDGEMENTS

This book has been written because of a number of persons. Some of them close by, some of them a bit further away.

First of all I want to thank Roy Martina and Brigitte Sumner, my mentor and coach, for their immense support during this personal journey of mine, helping me to finish this book.

Next I would like to thank Henri van Amerongen and Michael Coers, who have introduced me into the world of regression and hypnotherapy.

I'd like to thank Kees Goedegebure and John Chapman. Kees for helping me with the lay-out and the messages that have helped me make this journey. John for checking the translation!

Also I'd like to thank Kees Buursink for his inspiration to write the first note to the reader and helping me go on this journey fulltime!!!

Also, a big thank you to all my clients and friends who have inspired me to write this book and going on this journey and as a result guiding others.

Jackie Wright and Matthew Smith, thank you for your inspirational words with regards to my book-writing!!!

Natalie and Rekha… Need I say more?

Mom and Dad† (, Sis and Bro), I know you are so proud of me!!!

Nisandeh Neta, Eelco de Boer and Brendon Burchard, thank you all for sharing your knowledge and making this journey possible!

Last but not least I'd like to say thank you to my husband Nico for his never-ending support. Without him I would never have had the time to write this book and keep developing all things related.

A Big HUG and a Big SMILE ☺ to All of You!!!

Elise

FINALLY

This book is the first part in the series "Dreamin' Your Leadership". It describes a journey which will help you see what luggage and survival mechanisms you've been colleting during your life and what you might be able to do to let go off this luggage and fix those mindsets. It also explains the theory behind mindsets.

The follow-up to this book will be "Manifesting Your Leadership". This will be a workbook, which will help you to start working on your own luggage and mindsets by means of questions, assignments and of course some explanations when needed.

Also there will be a number of workshops and courses around the themes "Dreamin' Your Leadership" and "Manifesting Your Leadership". For more information please check www.ChikaraCC.com.

ABOUT THE AUTHOR

Elise A.C. Ledderhof (*writer's nickname Lexje) works as a Leadership Counsellor.

She guides other people to find their strengths and as a result take personal leadership. To do so, she helps them discover their blocking survival mechanism and transform this into a powerful mindset.

This book is describes a journey, during which memories start to surface about dreams and events that have made us into who we are today. When we decide it's time for change and start pursuing our dreams, it's important to leave behind certain baggage and burdens. We can then replace those by new support mechanisms, helping us to succeed. This book is an introduction on how to do so. It's been written as if you're part of an adventure yourself, keeping you intrigued from beginning to end.

Brigitte Sumner*, writer, entrepreneur coach, trainer and speaker- Turnaround Coaching & Consultancy Ltd. Great Brittan:*

This book is inspiring with yet a serious note. Things which seem futile are discussed, turning out to have a serious impact on your life. The good news is however that by using these insights, you have the ability to adjust your future and live the way you want to. Elise has stated now and for ever that you have the choice to live your life the way you want to. She applies this in her life as well, successfully.

Roy Martina*, holistic doctor, international bestseller author, trainer and speaker and develop of the revolutionary method Omega Healing:*

Lexje is a 5D dreamer with 3D results. Her talent is to manifest in a creative manner, meaning she activates her Right side of the brain, which can think in 5D and then realize this in the real 3D World. This course will teach you the basic principles to manifest whatever it is you want.*

ISBN 978-1-105-61880-2 90000
9 781105 618802

www.ingramcontent.com/pod-product-compliance
Ingram Content Group UK Ltd.
Pitfield, Milton Keynes, MK11 3LW, UK
UKHW020236250726
13967UKWH00001B/394

9 781105 618802